Anne Hatona
(christmas 95)

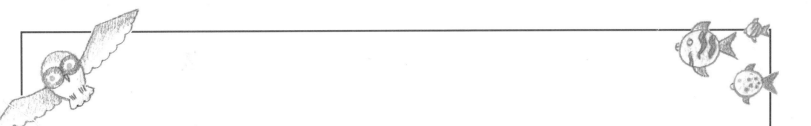

What shall I draw?

Ray Gibson

Designed and illustrated by Amanda Barlow

Edited By Felicity Everett

Series Editor: Jenny Tyler

Contents

Draw a pig

1 2 3 4

5 6 7 8

Lying down pig

1 2 3 Erase this line. 4

Sideways pig

1 2 3

A piggy scene

You could draw any kind of flowers. These are tulips.

For lettuce leaves, draw wiggly green shapes.

Green spikes for grass

Wavy brown lines for mud

Now how about... a pig family at dinner time?

Draw a sea monster

1

2

3

4

A sea monster battle

Soft blue
crayoning
for the sky

Drops of water

5

6

Draw a
pattern on
his body.

7

Draw a cloud.

Draw
sharp
teeth.

Draw a snail

1

2

3

4

5

6

Crayon in the body.

7

8

Make a pattern on the shell.

Draw the children

Draw some little baby snails.

Make the shells different.

Make a picture story

1

2

3

Draw snails on a flower.

Add some grass and leaves.

Open mouth

Jagged bite in the leaf

4

5

6

Draw a space rocket

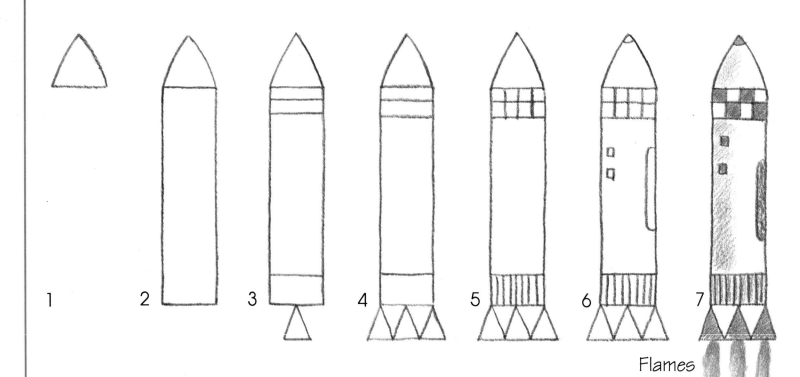

1   2   3   4   5   6   7

Flames

A rocket launch

1 Draw a tall ladder for the launch tower.

2

3

Add zig zag lines.

Dots for sparks

Add clouds of grey smoke.

Draw circles for planets. Crayon them brightly.

Spacewalker

Decorate the rocket.

You could add doors, windows, stripes or numbers.

Add tiny stars.

Now how about... a rocket on a strange planet?

Draw an owl

Start with a branch.

1

2

3

4

Draw a dot here.

5

6

7

8

9

10

Draw scribbly stripes on the wings.

11

Shade around the eyes.

12

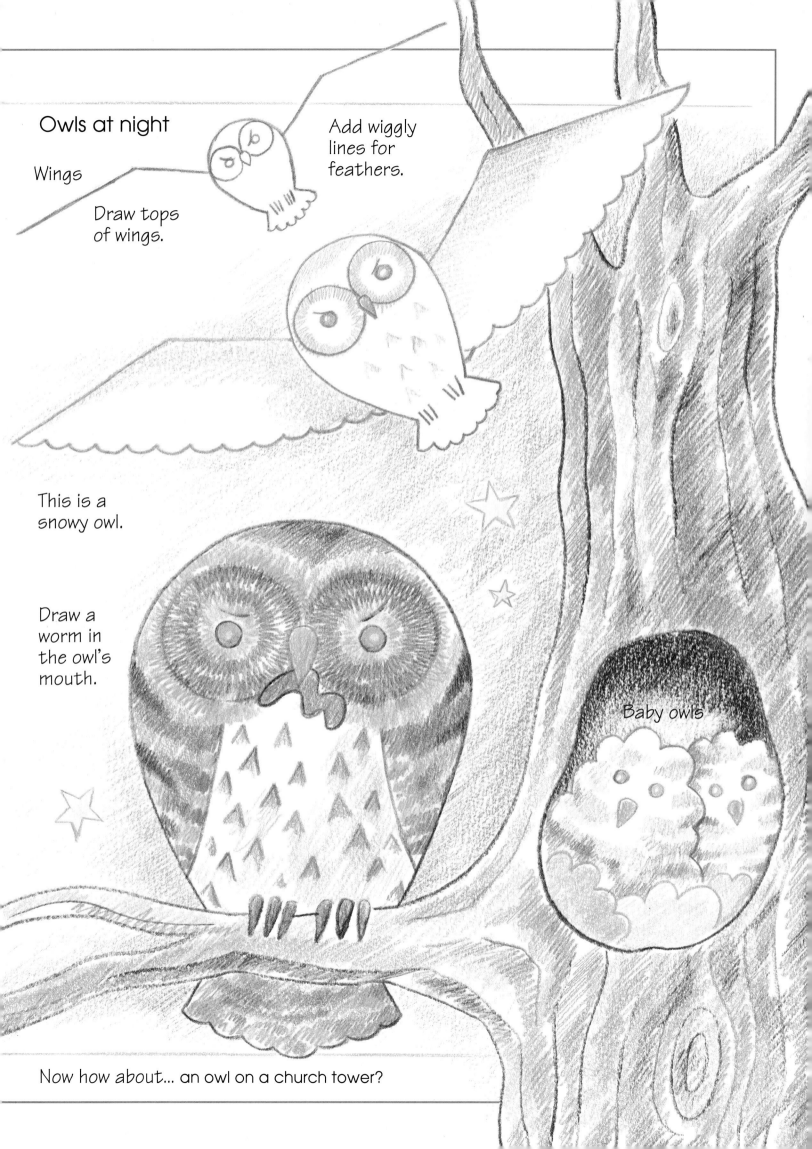

Owls at night

Wings

Draw tops
of wings.

Add wiggly
lines for
feathers.

This is a
snowy owl.

Draw a
worm in
the owl's
mouth.

Baby owls

Now how about... an owl on a church tower?

Draw a submarine

1

2

3 — Conning tower

4

5 Propellers

6 Hydroplanes

7

8

Under the sea

Draw a battle with a giant
octopus. Add sea creatures,
shells and seaweed.

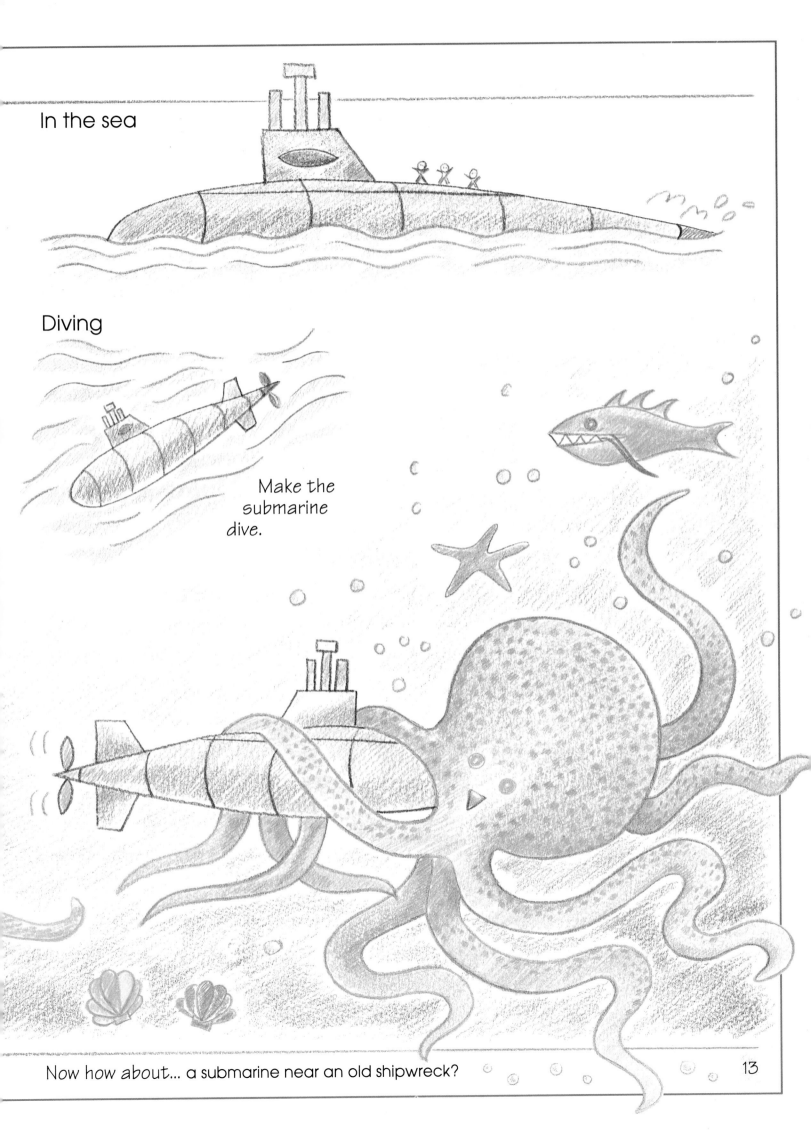

In the sea

Diving

Make the submarine dive.

Now how about... a submarine near an old shipwreck?

Draw a tiger

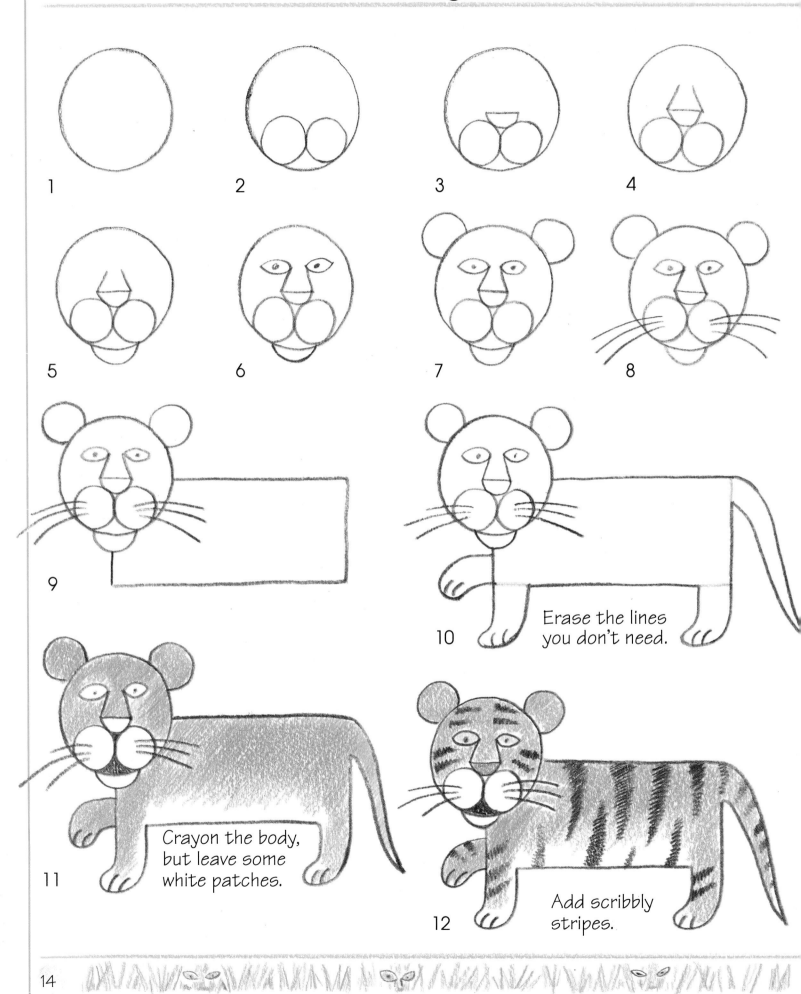

1

2

3

4

5

6

7

8

9

10 Erase the lines you don't need.

11 Crayon the body, but leave some white patches.

12 Add scribbly stripes.

Sleeping tiger

Leaping tiger

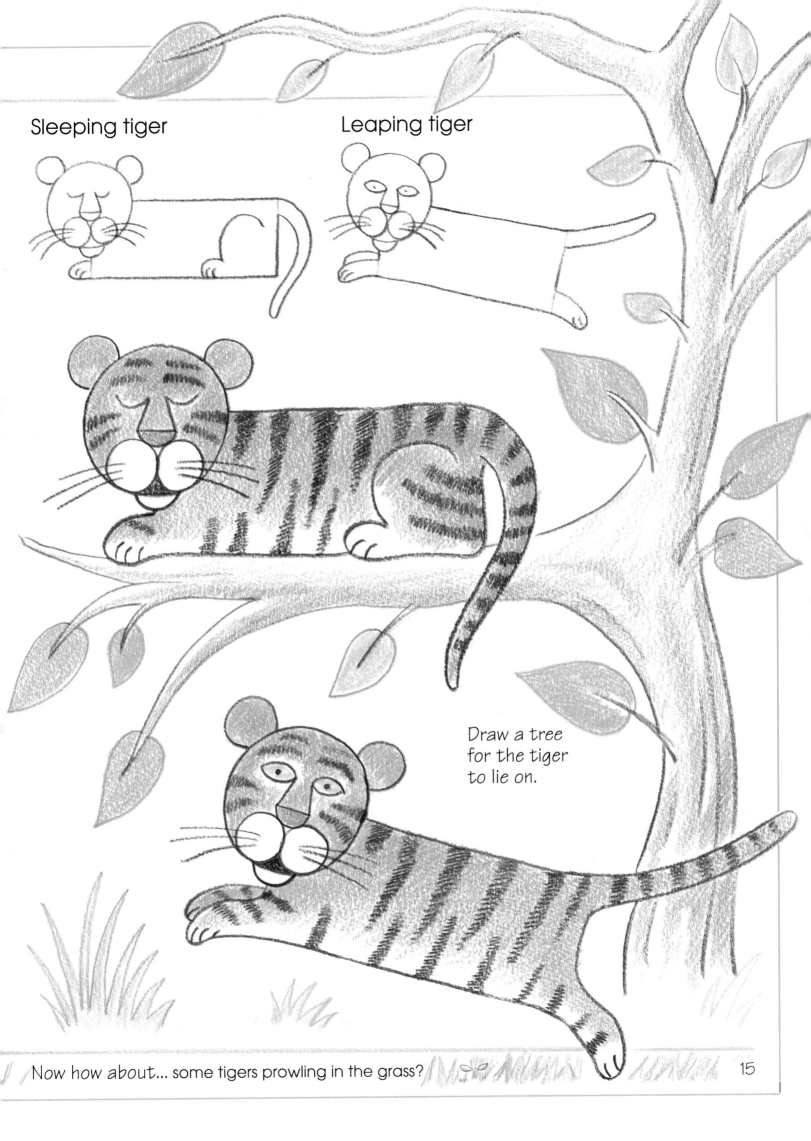

Draw a tree
for the tiger
to lie on.

Draw a wizard

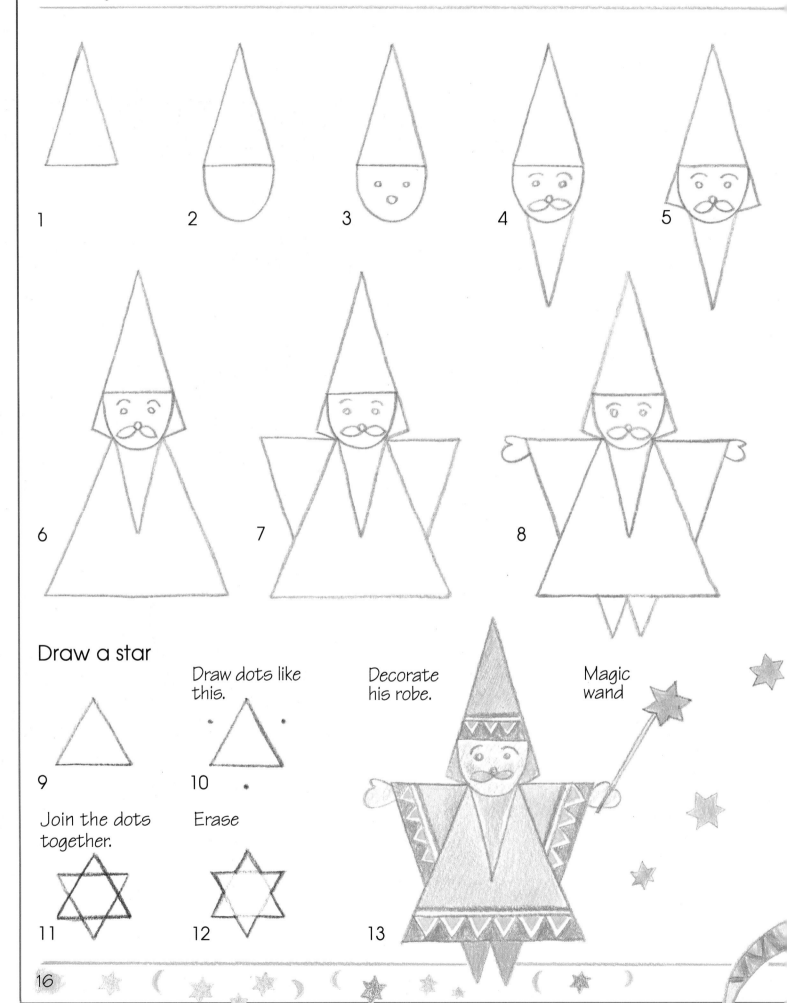

1

2

3

4

5

6

7

8

Draw a star

Draw dots like this.

9

10

Join the dots together.

Erase

11

12

13

Decorate his robe.

Magic wand

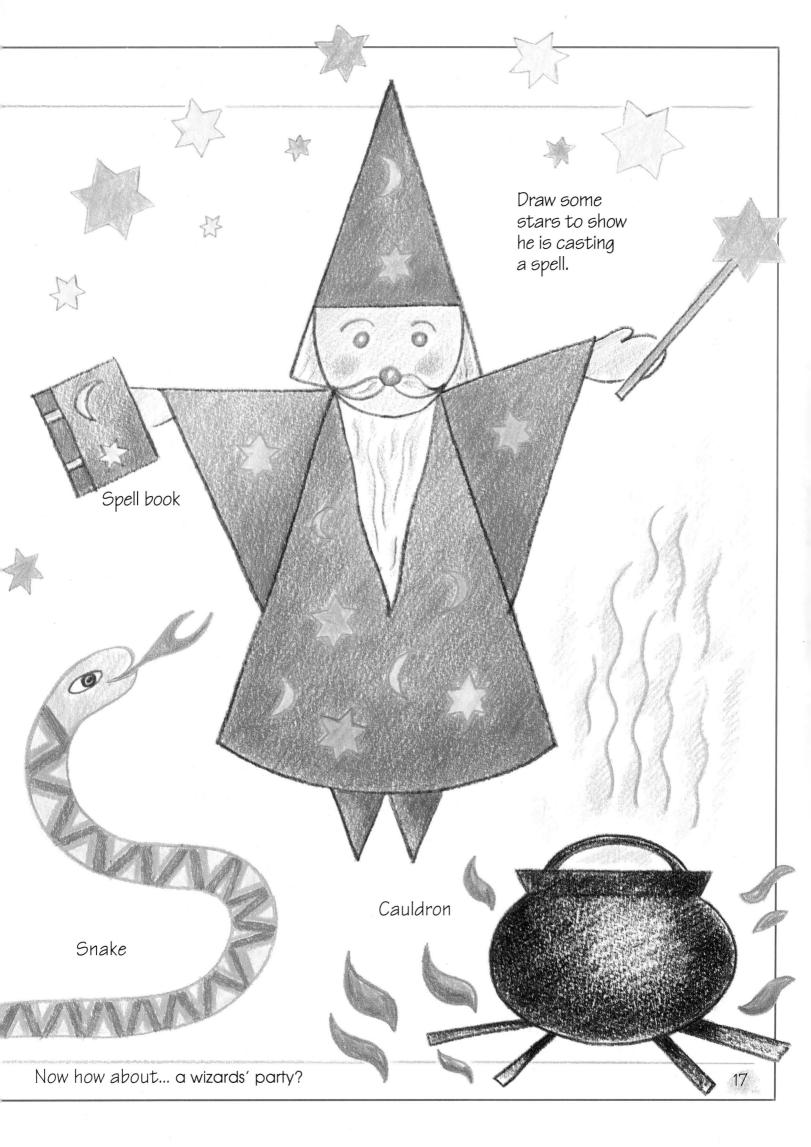

Draw some stars to show he is casting a spell.

Spell book

Snake

Cauldron

Draw a helicopter

1

2

3

4

5

6

Lines around the tail propeller make it seem to move.

7

8

Crayon your helicopter.

More flying 'copters

These helicopters are rescuing people.

This one has skids underneath, so it can land on the water.

Draw any patterns you like.

This helicopter is carrying logs.

Add some birds.

Draw the propellers like this when they are not moving.

Now how about... a helicopter landing on a skyscraper?

19

Draw a cat

Snoozing cat

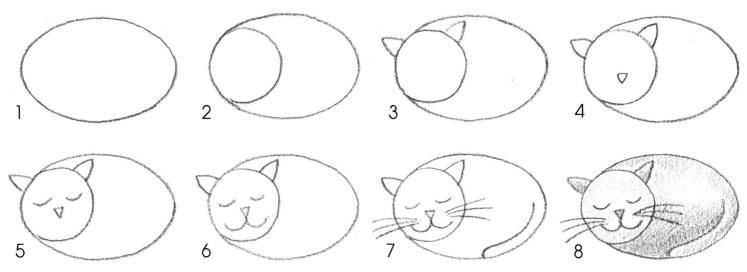

1
2
3
4

5
6
7
8

Standing cat

1
2
3
4

Crouching cat

1

Draw the body
in pencil first.

2

Erase one end.
Draw in the head.

Lapping cat

Add a
tongue and
a saucer of
milk.

3

Sitting cat

1

2

3

4

Cat family

Draw a large
sitting cat
for the
mother.

Comfy cat

Draw the snoozing cat
on a cushion.

Don't
forget
their
tails.

Now draw the kittens.
Add two paws beneath
each head.

Draw a box for the kittens.

Now how about... a cat on a roof...a cat chasing a mouse?

Draw circles

Dinner

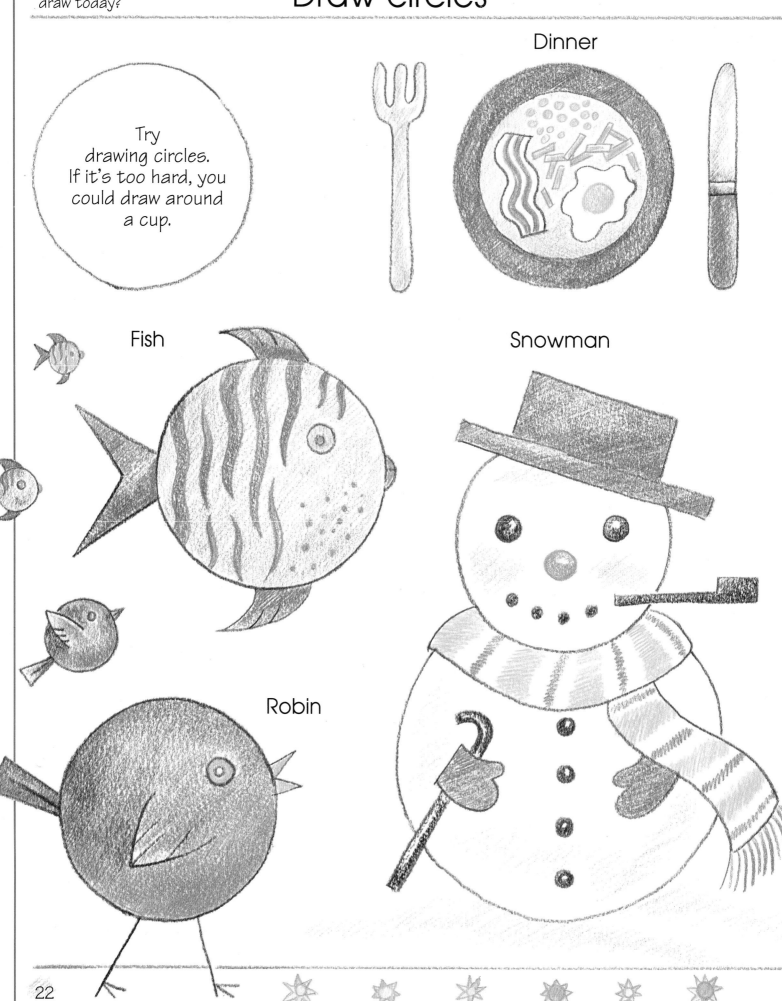

Try drawing circles. If it's too hard, you could draw around a cup.

Fish

Snowman

Robin

Apple

Clock

Balloon

Mouse

Lion

Now how about... a spider?... what else can you think of?

23

Draw a clown

1

2

3

4

5

6   Erase this line.

7

8

Clowning around

You could draw the arms in different positions.

Decorate the clown however you like.

Add some balls for a juggling clown.

Draw a ballerina

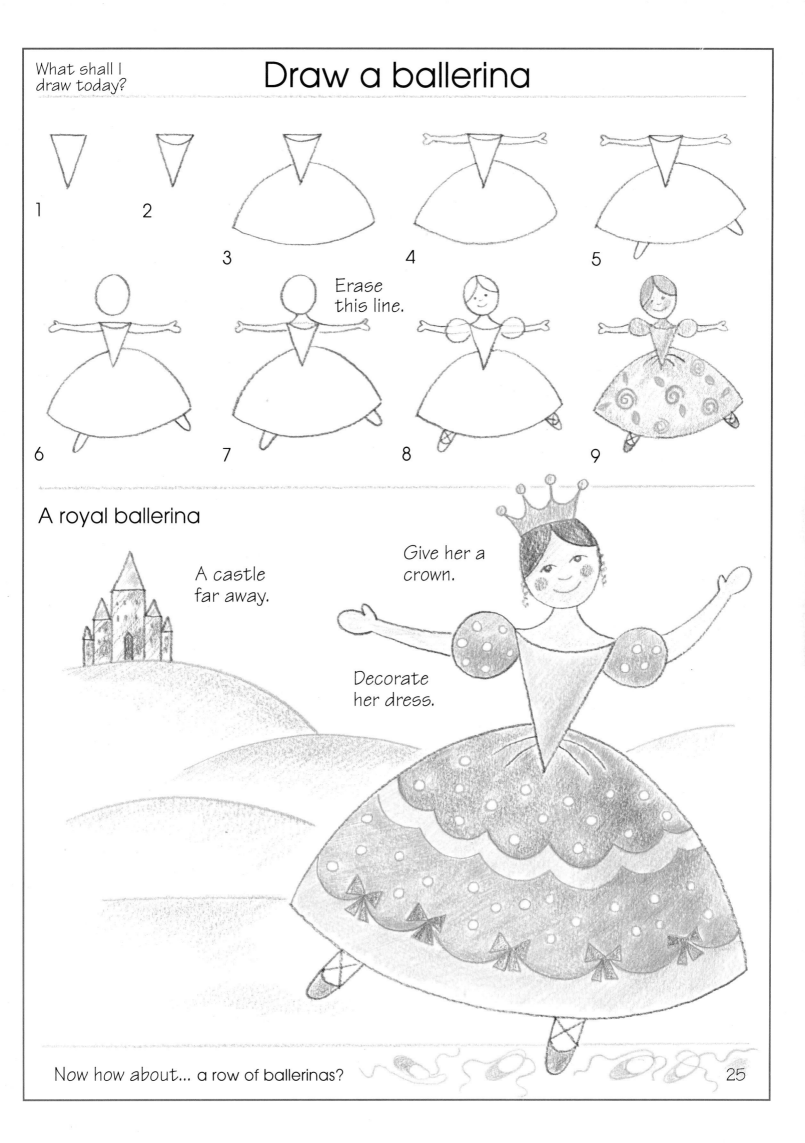

1

2

3

4

5

6

7

Erase this line.

8

9

A royal ballerina

A castle far away.

Give her a crown.

Decorate her dress.

Now how about... a row of ballerinas?

25

Draw a teddy

1

2

3

4

5

6

7

8

9

Walking Teddy

Erase the
lines you
don't
need.

Sitting teddy

Erase the
lines you
don't need.

Shouting teddy

Draw the
mouth open.

26

Teddy
bears'
picnic

Teddies
playing

Shading
for
straight
fur

Squiggles
for curly
fur

Now how about... teddy bears at a swimming pool?

Draw a castle

Leave gaps here

1

2

3

4

5

6

7

8

9

Flags

Windows

Crayon your castle.

10 Draw lines going across.

11 Add lines going down.

A castle on fire

Red and
orange flames

Add clouds
of smoke.

Make all the flames
go the same way.

Wiggly blue lines
for the castle moat

Buckets of water

Now how about... a castle in a storm with lightning?

Draw a pick-up truck

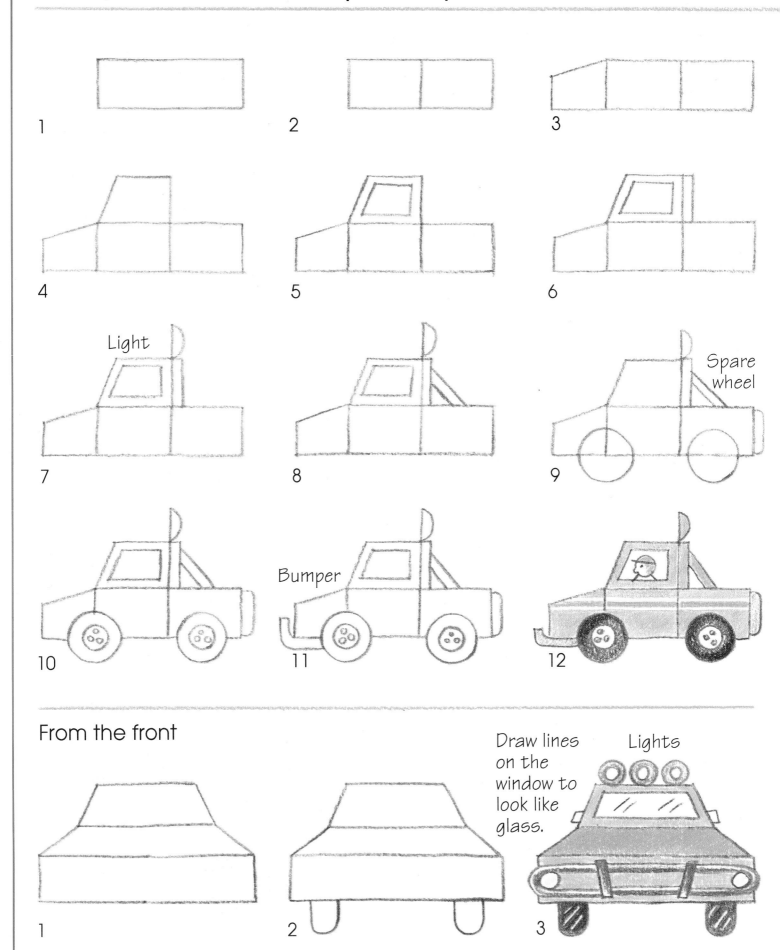

1

2

3

4

5

6

Light

7

8

Spare wheel

9

10

Bumper

11

12

From the front

1

2

Draw lines on the window to look like glass.

Lights

3

Draw a car

Headlights

Crayon your car.

1

2

Hub-caps

3

Pick up trucks at work

Draw a pick-up truck pulling a car out of a lake.

Add scenery

Pick-up trucks can go up steep slopes.

Now how about... a pick-up truck rescuing a racing car?

Things to do with your drawings

Mounting

1

Take a piece of paper or cardboard, a little bigger than your drawing.

2

Spread glue thinly over the back of the drawing. Put it in the middle of the mount.

3

With clean hands, smooth your drawing down firmly.

Fancy mounts

Cut a wiggly edge for your mount with scissors.

Decorate your mount with wrapping paper.

Draw a simple pattern on your mount.

Sprinkle glitter on your mount or stick on shiny stars.

Making a shaped card

Fold a piece of cardboard in half. Stick your drawing close to the fold. Leaving the folded side, cut around your drawing, close to the edge.